So BJÖRED

THE INNER THOUGHTS
OF UNIMPRESSED TOTS

RUNNING PRESS
PHILADELPHIA · LONDON

© 2015 by Running Press
Published by Running Press,
A Member of the Perseus Books Group

All rights reserved under the Pan-American and International Copyright Conventions
Printed in China

Books published by Running Press are available at special discounts for bulk purchases in the United States by corporations, institutions, and other organizations. For more information, please contact the Special Markets Department at the Perseus Books Group, 2300 Chestnut Street, Suite 200, Philadelphia, PA 19103, or call (800) 810-4145, ext. 5000, or e-mail special.markets@perseusbooks.com.

ISBN 978-0-7624-5753-3
Library of Congress Control Number: 2015938694

E-book ISBN 978-0-7624-5804-2

9   8   7   6   5   4   3   2   1
Digit on the right indicates the number of this printing

Designed by Jason Kayser
Edited by Jennifer Leczkowski
Typography: Mija

Running Press Book Publishers
2300 Chestnut Street
Philadelphia, PA 19103-4371

Visit us on the web!
www.runningpress.com

For Jack.

Introduction

· · · · · · · · · · · · ·

These days, babies are everywhere—in the park, at the mall, on the beach, in the seat behind you on that 5-hour flight. You might even have a baby in your own home!

If you've ever met a baby, then you know that there's much more to them than meets the eye. They aren't just burping, drooling, poop machines. They are complicated and temperamental creatures with unique personalities. But sometimes it can be tough to figure out what's going on in their cute little wobbly noggins.

Parents try all kinds of things to please or entertain them, but the babies are not amused. In fact, they're pretty unimpressed. So they got together to write this book, to tell us what they really think. Okay, babies didn't write this book, but somebody did. And that somebody used to be a baby, so that must count for something.

Hmm,
thought the
view would be
better.

Is that a tinge of excitement
I'm feeling? Nope, just gas.

I find the term "cry-baby" kind of insulting.

Great, a road trip.
Let me guess—
Grandma's house
again?

I learned to smile a while ago. I only do it when you leave the room.

Just counting down
the minutes until naptime.

A-B-C-D-OMG,
H-I-J-K-LMAO-P...

I'm sure
all three of
your followers
on Instagram will
get a kick
out of this.

I'm not sure what's more irritating: my diaper rash or your baby talk voice.

I guess I'm a bottle-is-half-empty kind of guy.

Hold on a sec, I have to text
my imaginary friend.

As the leaves wither away and winter's chill approaches, I can't help but ponder my own mortality.

They can take my freedom,
but they can never take my binky.

This thing where the clouds pee on everything—I like this.

Apathy is wasted
on the old.

I feel a little overwhelmed.
I could really use a
time-out.

Watching grass grow is
an underappreciated pastime.

Ugh—on hold with tech support again.

I haven't had
this much fun since
that time I had the
hiccups for an
hour and a half.

I scream, you scream, then I scream some more.

I'm not a fan of Mondays...
or whatever today is.

I need a new
baby sister
like I need another
circumcision.

I see you settled on Porpoise Gray for the nursery walls. Bold choice.

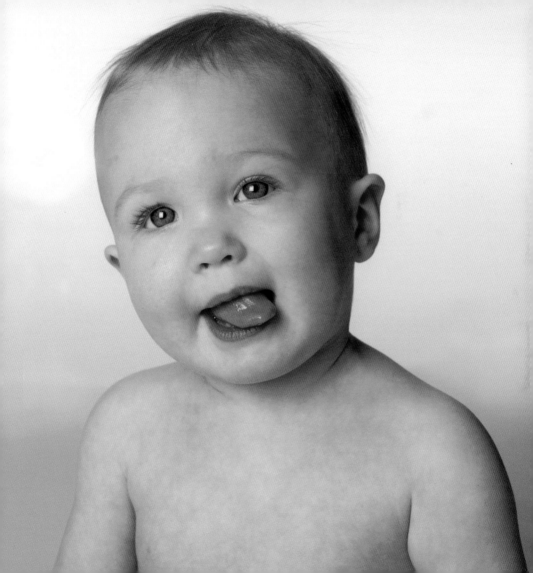

I can't feel my legs. Aside from that I'm having an awful time.

I'm saving the drama
for my mama.

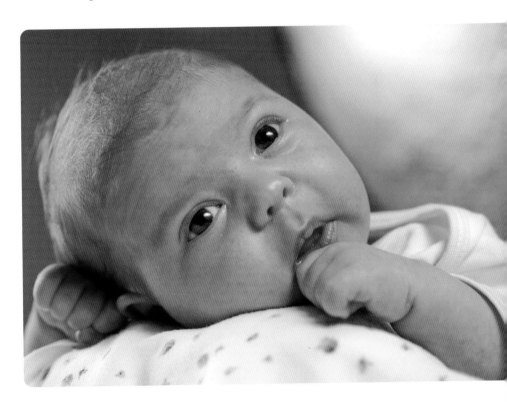

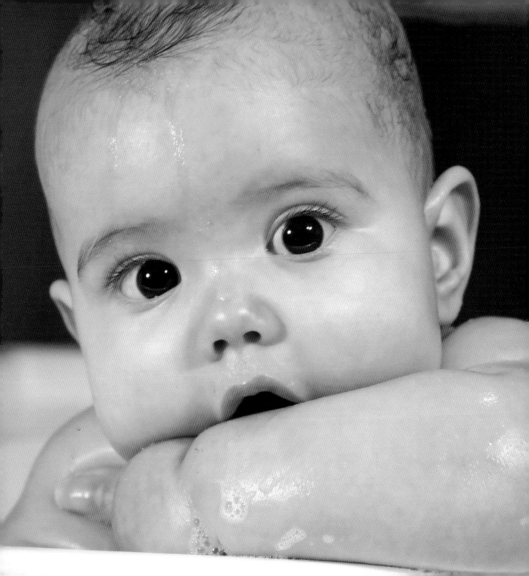

Sometimes I like to take a bath with the lights turned down and imagine I'm back in the womb. Those were good times.

Don't tell the
tall ones,
but I like you best,
fuzzy brother.

Okay, I think you've reached
your daily kiss quota.

Excuse me if I'm cranky—I've only had 13 hours of sleep today.

I don't care.
You see, my frontal lobe
is still developing so I
don't yet have the
mental capacity to care.
But even if I could care,
I wouldn't care.

Don't mind me, I'm just experiencing an existential crisis.

Could we go out in public once
without you embarrassing me?

Here's one for the scrapbook—
baby's first frown.

Instead of counting sheep, I count my disappointments.

I see you
splurged on a designer
diaper bag.
Do the words
"college fund" mean
anything to you?

How about you put down the
camera and grab me a napkin?

I'll talk when I have something nice to say. It might be a while.

On the bright side, the spit-up stain on your blouse draws attention away from your bloodshot eyes.

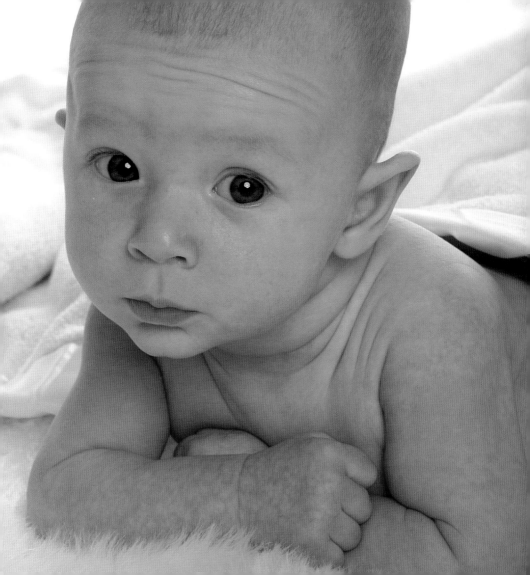

So it just makes a dumb noise? I can't check my Twitter with it?

If I say "mama" will you leave me alone for five minutes?

I spaced out for a minute there—
what were you saying?

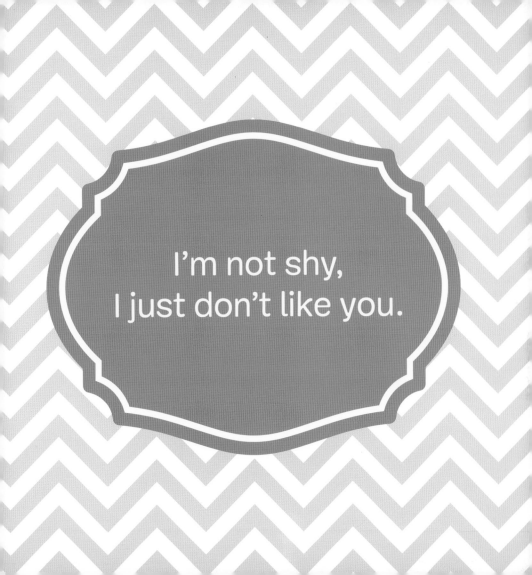

I know you have
an important meeting
in the morning, but I
think I want to stay up all
night screaming.
You might want to make
some coffee.

How lovely.
Can we go home now?

Cool it with the airplane noises.
You're not fooling anyone.

I slept like a
baby last night.
I woke up five times.
And I pooped
myself.

This little piggy
is going up your
nose if you don't quit
playing with
my feet.

Hey Warden—
is it chow time yet?

For how long does this "babysitter" intend to sit on me?

Do you really think making me listen to Beethoven's 5th will make me smarter? Everyone knows his 9th symphony is where it's at.

All this singing about falling cradles is going to give me nightmares.

Is my hairline receding or is it just the lighting in here?

Bundle of joy?
Whatever you say.

This is the worst
day of my life.
Of course,
it's the only day of
my life.

I see you've stolen my nose.
Well played, Mommy.

Double
your displeasure.

My parents decided to dress me as a humiliated baby for Halloween.

I think I
need to take a
break
from carbs.

My wish is for this
unpleasant soiree to end.

Could you scoot over?
You're in my light.

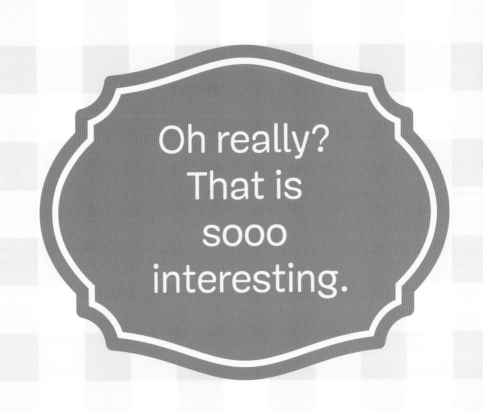

Oh really?
That is
sooo
interesting.

Tummy time? More like *crummy* time, amirite??

I can barely contain my enthusiasm.

You mean
to tell me your
name isn't
really Mom?

Nose... itches... must... escape...

Fresh air is
totally overrated.

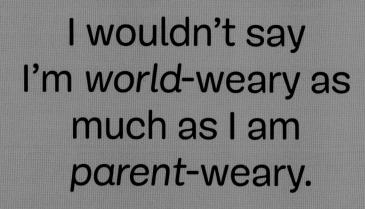

I wouldn't say I'm *world*-weary as much as I am *parent*-weary.

Oh, you're still
running Windows 7?
Interesting...

All aboard!
Next stop: Dullsville.

Am I supposed to be
amused?

I suppose
this is what they
mean by
"having a ball."

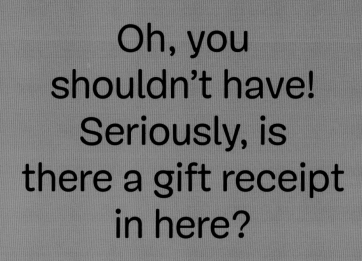

Oh, you shouldn't have! Seriously, is there a gift receipt in here?

Whoa... How many bottles
did I have last night?

When did life become such a chore?

Yes! I made them
all disappear!

Photo Credits

• • • • • • • • • • • •

They all lived happily ever after?
How utterly predictable.